Our
Master
Plan

Books by Dara Wier _____

Blook, Hook & Eye
The 8-Step Grapevine
All You Have in Common
The Book of Knowledge
Blue for the Plough
Our Master Plan

Our Master Plan

poems by Dara Wier

1975   1999

Twenty-Five Years of Publishing
Carnegie Mellon University Press

Acknowledgments _____

Grateful acknowledgment is made to the editors of the
following publications in which these poems first appeared:

American Poetry Review, "Apologies For and Further Explana-
tion to Divert Accusations of Equivocation"; *Black Warrior
Review*, "After the Birds Learned to Count to Eight," "Reflec-
tions Upon Sitting, Along with a Friend, for an Itinerant
Painter, Manitoba, 1938"; *Boulevard*, "The White Boat";
Conduit, "The Soup Drill," "One Hand Short"; *Crab Orchard
Review*, "Resolution," "Company"; *Cutbank*, "Enough Said," "I
Remember Rilke"; *The Gettysburg Review*, "The Cubist
Rotisserie," "Untitled"; *Harvard Review*, "Interview"; *Heat*
(Australia) "The White Boat," "Apologies For and Further
Explanation to Divert Accusations of Equivocation," "No
Clue"; *The Iowa Review*, "A Secret Life," "5 1/2 Inch Lullaby";
Meanjin (Australia), "Interview," "5 1/2 Inch Lullaby"; *North
Stone Review*, "The Lost Pastor"; *Overland* (Australia),
"Enough Said"; *Salt* (Australia), "The Long Story"; *The Seattle
Review*, "All in a Day's Work"; *The Southern Review*, "Any-
thing You Find of Mine Is Yours."

"Fly on the Wall" appeared as a limited edition chapbook
published in 1996 by Oat City Press, East Providence, Rhode
Island.

The author is grateful to the John Simon Guggenheim Foundation.

Publication of this book is supported by a grant from the Pennsylvania
Council on the Arts.

Library of Congress Catalog Card Number 97-76753
ISBN 0-88748-293-7
ISBN 0-88748-294-5 Pbk.

10 9 8 7 6 5 4 3 2 1

Contents

for Emily
for Guy
for Jim

From all I did and all I said
let no one try to find out who I was.
— C. P. Cavafy

The White Boat

The birds are sleeping, it's far from morning,
except for the birds who rightfully haunt
the dark, and the low-life, lazy geese
who've given up their fly-way rights
to live at ease around the man-made pond
below the ridge. They come around the hour
of the wolf and wake me up. I can't help but
love their haunting, honking grief.
It sounds like grief tonight.
A white boat in full moon light is rocking
on the lawn. It rocks and rocks
like a giant's cradle or a mammoth's bassinet.
It rocks like a cradle for a god or a devil.
The white boat doesn't want to go home.

Apology for and Further Explanation of an Attempt to Divert Accusations of Equivocation

In my hometown it was like January,
like January in Oaxaca, in Fortin

de las Flores, like Fortin
in the mid-forties, like the 40s

in December, like December
on the river, a forest of willows

half in, half out of water,
like the river in the picture,

like the picture above your bureau,
like your bureau filled to over-flowing

with feathers every color of the spectrum
feathers blown through vowels,

through curtains of bougainvillea, going
on forever, forever as it formerly was,

in the lustre of a loved one's luggage,
baggage to carry lightly or solemnly

toss off into the Bay of Fundy.
Thank you for four golden mice

who never wake me up at night,
for the pocket-size surveillance device,

for books which tell me nothing's unakin.
In January it was like my hometown

in the 1940s in the middle of December,
December a cool glass of water at noon

in the summer, a clinking of cowbells
to signal it's evening. I was seven,

four, eight, eleven, still unborn,
brother to my younger sister,

sister to my mother, father like a twin,
twins like vapor trails on clear nights

in October. You were my shadow
I dared not step into. You stood by

my shoulder, champion, angel, faithful
companion I dared not look in the eye.

What was it like for you?
Were you about to step into your skin,

like water poured from a pitcher,

like an ant into amber, like molten gold?

Was the gold like someone's fortune
or folly, folly a moving picture you'd get

into for a quarter, when a quarter meant
more than a dollar, a dollar a bit

of a future you'd be expected to furnish,
I'd be with you to finish,

of a finish wearing the date of your birth,
polished with everyone's hopes,

polished with everyone's dreams,
lost in a basket of keepsakes.

5 1/2 Inch Lullaby

When something he would never know,
when something happened to him
when he was too young to remember,
when it reminded him,
when he knew all along,
when someone lies about something,
when it doesn't mean it isn't true,
when he was too young to remember,
when he was sleepy and friendly with thoughts,
when he'd spent the day gathering,
when his head touched his pillow,
when he was too young to remember,
when it stood among his towns, runways, train-
        routes and farms,
when each animal had a name, a place
        and a purpose,
when it remained as he made it,
when he wanted to change it,
when something confused and cluttered
        everything he'd spent the day building,
when his jetfighters sank in his rivers,
when his frogs on their lilypads floated
        to the tops of his tilting skyscrapers
when he was finally falling asleep,
when his room floated above the other rooms,
when noises and music and voices rose,
when the legionnaire stays true to his dream,

when another goes on and on,
when a tone without words takes on form,
when the wonders of everything wear down,
someone steps in the room.

Interview

What was it you first noticed?
I found her stupified, in the oven,
dumbfounded, stunned, in her oven.
And then? Then I found her again,
tasting a shoe she'd baked.
How did you feel? I had no words
for that. I hadn't felt
anything approaching it.
Can you describe anything else?
Can you say anything more about,
about how you felt when you knew?
I didn't know.
Can you say something more, something
about the way you felt about it?
It continually interrupted me,
anything I might have felt.
I was absorbed.
Then what, what happened next?
She began licking her hands, no, first
it was her eyes, she'd touch them.
And then? Then what was left?
I don't know. I wanted to lend her
something, though whatever that
might have been is lost to me.
Did you keep track of her activities?
No, yes, well, they were eradicating.
Well, let's go back

to specifics. Can you say
anything about her habits?
She'd lost that thought. She had none.
She had none? She floated? Uh, huh,
every day there were plans to consider.
Plans? Yes. What sort of plans?
A nail had come loose from a vortex
she'd driven. The tread on the tires
wore away. Something about filters.
It was an idea under siege.
Under siege? Embattled. You understand,
nothing I wanted to say could help.

Fly on the Wall

Back in the 30s he'd done his bit,
making big money in the sci-fi camp,
squirrelling it away in real estate scams
and rare books.
I'd flown in for his annual solstice party
to watch him do his party trick.
He'd rigged his party lights to flick on and off
with just the touch of his fingertip
on a snake plant's stalk.
I could walk all night long over the same surface
with absolutely zero effect.
His guest list was never long,
enormous twins in sea green satin gowns
with phosphorescent tiaras on,
a string bean of a man in a skintight suit,
lugging around a nose-making kit,
a troop of brownies with stethoscopes,
killing jars, relaxing chambers and insect pins.
I was feeling queasy and my heart beat poorly.
But the old commander always sensed
my unnerved concern and invited me down
into his rare book room.
He showed me the broken spines of books he loved
and books he'd never sell. He told me stories
about men and women who jerked books around,
who shouted and screamed at books,
who breathed on them.
He whispered to me tales of books
he'd seen lying in gutters

and books used for doorstops and paperweights.
He showed me a book wrapped in cellophane,
its pages uncut, its binding sharp as his eyes,
and said it had been the murder weapon
in an ancient assassination.
He told me about my cousins who eat books,
glue, paper and ink, and stand on the library's steps
and brag and give speeches about it.
He did not seem surprised
that I should have never known
how many bugs live in books all their lives.
He pointed to a book in which it is written
how one pair of flies, left to their own desires,
will produce 25 generations of offspring
in fewer than 365 days. Our numbers, if left unchecked,
could increase to fill a ball 96 million miles wide.
My kind of flies!
Flies, he breathed, with no time for books.
He went on telling me how most people treat books
like bricks, how most books stand lonely and unread
on dirty shelves, cities for spiders,
ballast for drifters, seasonal gifts,
touched barely once and forgotten.
He brought out books faded by the light of day
and books strong as giants
that broke other books down,
that bullied other books into submission,
and a few that stood firm in any circumstance

protecting weak and sick books
that could not defend themselves.
He pulled down *The Insect World of Henri Fabre*
and let me crawl over its tender insinuations.
A crisp, uncirculated twenty dollar bill
fell to the floor from page 20.
We stared at it, my old friend and I,
the way galaxies gaze upon history.
I hauled myself into the safety of the depths
of his trousers' rolled cuff
and we crept up the steps to ride out
the rest of the party. The ladies in green
crooned old lullabies to the brownies.
Every nose in the galley was set right on its face.
I clung to the wall and thought of the stranger
who'd wielded a book to flatten my mother.
While the cold evening turned into morning
the old commander palpated his party lights
and cranked up his old victrola.
I flew to his side and stood like a dog
by his master. We listened to secrets
that pass between strangers
who've spent the evening eyeing each other.
A loaded sailor in earmuffs strolled near
and looked me over. Hey, flyweight, he muttered,
who do you think you are?
Who me, I faltered, me, I'm nobody,

I'm the half-deaf fly on the wall.
The commander fluffed my bristles, tapped
my orbital plate and adjusted my crooked antennae.
He shooed me toward the transom
out of the way of my incessant fate.
Tomorrow would last a few minutes longer.

Don't Say My Name

Skull, axis, kernel of focus,
hub of center, genius of crisis,

brain, swaddled in silken tufts,
shawl, veil, scarf, majestic loft.

Listing, harebrained, keeling,
right-side-up and up-side-down,

one big lonesome brain searching
through eternity for eyes, arms, legs,

forty acres and a mule,
kind neighbors, good luck, faithful

lover. Big, guileless baby of a brain
searching through eternity

with cracks in its skull
nerve-endings escape,

attracting bees like honey,
lightning bolts like thoughts,

nerve-endings like smoky moths.
What fool thinks of strands

of hair as passing thoughts?
Who wants to comb them all

morning and stroke them back
to sleep all night?

Whose hands haven't
felt as if they've detached

to careen through space
like stray thoughts of a lost planet,

searching through space for your hair,
to touch it, to worship its source?

After the Absence of Sound Appears the Presence of Material

If sound can be broken,
and it will be,
and broken into over and over
again in visible syllables
dropped from vaults of glass domes,
sound can stand still
as it has to, so what is still
must be gone away from
to be wanted more.
Who hears a scrap of thought
can't help listening for the next,
put this with that,
put it over this
loved one's voice,
moist as it fills in notches
silence hacks away.
Scissors into silk.
Wood speaks to mud,
milk against tooth,
swimming up from depths
too deep to rise above.
Why go there?
Where the sign points to before
it is always too late.
And then a sudden blast
after which everything is quiet.

Untitled

It gives us a chance to lean close to a friend,
to brush the simple crumb of chocolate

from his shirt before it melts.
Or it lets us touch a bead of sleep

a lover's eye protects.
It makes it possible to make a wish,

to see an eyelash prevent a car crash,
or keep what we love from harm's way.

It protects us as well from those creeps
who think of us as legal tender

in their private stock of fodder.
Oh, it can turn up as a fly in good soup, but

it was put there on purpose, by the cook.
It spins all of the everywhere unravelling

loose threads straight back to their spindle,
back through music, through time and space

and television and breakfast cereal, through
petroleum and photosynthesis each in its season.

It distributes chromosomes as if chromosomes

counted for something. And it costs us nothing.

It's as easily overlooked as Mars lights
or pistol grips. It's nothing like anything

you'd find in a footnote. Whoever even thinks
to steal it spontaneously combusts and leaves

all evidence and memory without a trace.
Whoever claims to name it loses his name

and the names of his ancestors and children
go up in smoke. It disturbs only those

for whom value equals the sum of cost, who
disturb sleeping dogs, on whom everything is lost.

It distributes itself regardless of age, class,
race, club affiliation or sex, food groups, genius

or reason. It can be found on page twenty-nine
of the book you're always telling someone to read.

Over all inquisitions, crusades, haircuts, contracts
and baptisms it witnesses. Ambulance chasers

and pornographers get their share right along
with the bystanders. It does not interfere

with anyone's career. It's there for the wars
and for the breaking of treaties, when half

the world's sleeping and the other half weeps.
It's up on the shelf in the back of the closet,

down in the cellar, down in the Titanic.
It drew you as close as you've ever come

to what you must fear. It's on the cuffs of technicians
when they fiddle with switches.

It stands by the executioner when he decides
what to wear.

A Secret Life

The not quite invisible flowers
on the farthest edges

of out-of-the-way meadows
should not speak of it.

And yet they listen.
Their spans of silent attention

embarrass ardent lovers.
Cats intent on unreachable sparrows

look dementedly distracted
compared to these faithful flowers.

Imaginary walls go down,
walls of re-inforced steel rise up,

walls of paper, plaster, walls
of ice, walls of brick, straw,

mud, gingerbread and glass.
The light-sensitive photo-optic,

technologically advanced wall of louvers
has a mind of its own.

It's useless to hope

to break its concentration.

When I returned I found four walls
surrounded by a new idea, a bakery.

I pretended to be hungry
for their bread and cakes

so I could go inside.
So many years had passed

the bakers didn't know me
or that my life had gone by inside

the rooms their fragrant ovens filled.
I imagined myself once again

entering the lives of saints and animals
who never failed to welcome me,

a long-lost sister, a stranger.
Our tenderness toward one another

never, never faltered.
My thoughts have hidden themselves

from everything available
which might have made them visible.

An evergreen hedge may take

half a woman's life to grow

and then what should she put inside--
a few plain, domestic anachronisms--

woodpiles, abandoned cars, clotheslines,
a necessary lie, a grave you should

have taken to the grave?
My terminally-ill neighbor hid

herself from me with rows of arborvitae.
I told myself she cared for me

enough to protect me from her misery.
Was that another lie?

Nothing can protect me
from what churns up inside.

My illness secreted itself
where none could bring themselves

to find it. So much of what we do
in secret we don't know we do.

We dream of what we really are
and spend lifetimes denying it.

That was just a dream

I say, forgetting it.

Dreams don't come true
says the empty bucket,

sloshing with imaginary water,
as it's hauled up by the hand

of a non-existent stranger
hoping to quench my infinite thirst.

Near the end of his life
Henry Adams spent an evening

telling his young niece all he knew
because she would not understand

a word of it and so would never
quote him. Poor Henry.

I Remember Rilke

I remember Rilke sopping wet,
sprawled out as usual
all over his lilac bed,
newfangled breezes firing up
his freezing rooms,
crumbs of sesame drugs
loose in his killer hair.
Like 91% of the rest of us
he lied about the time
he spent alone.
He spent most of his time
on the telephone.
And the rest in pursuit
of a spider he'd run across
at supper, striding up
his butter knife.
He was one handsome devil,
all tensile muscle
built for rapid travel.
He never once said please
or hesitated to crawl
into dinner plates.
Such a relief to see
a grown, living spider,
astride a trivet, declaiming
against minutiae, by simple

virtue of his bearing,
the unrequired champion
of infinity, enjoying himself
at the table, encouraging
Rilke to commit to memory
his adoration of a certain
shade of violet. Without
apology, without so much as
a nod toward regret, he ambled
up a woman's arm and turned
like a friendly bracelet around
her sensible wrist. I don't
remember truly much more about Rilke.

After the Birds Learned to Count to Eight

In any case everyone felt obligated
to have an opinion or at least an opinion
regarding your opinion if you had one.
Often enough passing thoughts evolved
into convictions. Some were etched in stone,
some decided to go it alone, many were suspended,
many stood up like feathers in our caps.
We were distant and we were near North America's
geographical center. It was never where
we thought it was. Our skullcaps, our secret
lubrications fooled the sun we bet on, the sun
we agreed stayed up there. All the old codgers
burrowed in nearby and held up hand-lettered
signs: No Signs of Life Found Here.
We took that to mean do something useful,
say signup for four-hand piano at least,
or something along those lines, requiring the use
of all of our fingers and most of our time.
We would also need a gazebo, an array of vendors,
(corn dogs, frozen bananas, fried frog, quail grog)
Hmong quilters, greenpeacers, sandal zealots,
a chamber of commerce, additional security and
fire personnel. We were to remain extemporaneous,
at all cost. But cost wasn't a factor, money
didn't matter! When we protested we had no talent
our music teachers protested back. Our teachers

lacked the requisite attacks of conscience.
They wanted to convince us we could be good.
They'd harmonize good's as good as a plain doorknob,
as they clunked our heads together to smart us
into devotional attitudes. So, all right, we'd perform
what we couldn't learn. Such stern teachers we had,
with soft hearts, too, so it got to be our job
to convince them they'd tried as hard as they could.
Straight A's for them. To their dismay, to their
apoplexy. Anyway, the midwives were mixing it up
with the morticians over punch bowls of galactic
proportions. One of the planets in our solar system
might be blown out of the water tomorrow.
And we thought it was our millenium.
We would all wear handsomely tailored life jackets
and cheer one another on with old camp songs.
Everyone would eat recently vintaged peas,
an industrial accident everybody praised.
The children just followed along, caught
in our wake, bobbing up and down like corks
in a great salt lake.

Enough Said

The stray cat had no tail.
The tooth didn't seem to matter.

I felt comfortable being mistaken.
I felt at ease.

Your cardinal is one thousand times
more handsome than mine.

Having seen your cardinal
I find mine downright gruesome,

not homely, mind you, anguished.
Soon we'll be vacuuming our cars,

soon we'll be standing up, walking
around, just like normal,

just like whipped cream. My cardinal's mate
is not all that pretty herself.

But she's got a brighter look about her
than the parched petunias.

Of course she's eating
and they are not, not quite.

Pretty soon we're going to find

whatever it is we're looking for.

A fine excess of sentimentality
is what cemeteries are for.

People should visit them
more often. Last night

after everyone was gone to sleep
I put on some music and talked

to myself. I suppose there's a name
for my condition.

Our friend, Jeanne, likes to tell
about her friend who tries to impress

everyone by plunging his egg-battered
hand into boiling oil.

Sorry, Jeanne, that doesn't wash.
I wash on Wednesdays and that's

traditional. From hatch to flight
baby birds spend somewhere, between

directory assistance, between hanging on
hold, between, oh, this is a ballpark

estimate, fifteen to twenty days,
depending on weather conditions

and availability of food, if they are
robins, species differ.

That's a good question.
What did you think it means?

It means in summer everyone relaxes
when they aren't answering questions

and working or running errands
or planning trips.

Some things are more rewarding
than others. That's a fact.

It's comforting to have a butterfly
fieldguide; the word survive is over-

used, trivialized. You can't be
too careful. Yesterday I saw a baby

squirrel running over the road,
up on the re-invented phone line.

At first I thought how dangerous.
Suppose it turns out all my second

thoughts are best? God knows,
I'd have one long uninterrupted thought.

And think of the bird who lights on it,
and pity the bird who lights on it,

and funny the bird who lights on it,
and amazing the bird who lights on it.

Company

Then there came the day my friends
did everything they did
at the same time together.
They looked exactly like one another.
I said it made me mad.
I meant it had me all confused.
Clothes, hats, cars, shoes, books, food,
all the same. I no longer knew who
might be who and received a good deal
of sympathy. They had me so confused.
Now I can barely arrange myself properly
for company. Most recently two of my friends
celebrated the day Coca Cola was invented.
That's a success story. All day they'd been
wanting hamburgers. Between friends
nothing is forbidden. They like mayonnaise,
lettuce, tomatoes, onions, on toast,
with roasted chilis and cheese.
The conversation revolved around horses.
About taking care of horses on their way
to slaughterhouses, about what a market
there is for horse in France, of course,
but also in Scandinavian countries where
they like their horse in sausage along with
eels in aspic. There's a discrete market
for horse in America which turns out to be
a forbidden topic. I didn't know veal

happens to be less prized in France than beef,
or that there is not now nor has there ever
been anything there we could call a ranch.
I loved all my friends even as they persisted
in tricking me, which amounted to telling me
the truth about everything all at once.
Pulses of weather disturbances encouraged me.
The sun shone on spring leaves, then it
hailed and the temperature dropped forty degrees.
Down to the minute, down to the man, everyone
agreed we must uncomplicate our lives.

Our Master Plan

Celeste goes waltzing with bears.
Natalie shops for milk glass on pedestals
modeled after the hoofs of baby goats.
Mr. Holdrogen whips in and out of his tuxedo
faster than a pileated woodpecker
can count without a calculator.
Mark and Peg corner the market on legible parakeets.
Spencer's attention to our master plan strays.
Pam invents a netherworldly new perfume.
We rule out Aperçu.
David monikers it, Template.
Peter knows the time has come to run as fast as he can.
Jean Marie finally adopts a highway,
mindboggling the numbers of chipmunks and squirrels
who survive her drive-by cleaning services.
Emily discovers a secret room adjoins the room
of her own.
Spencer stays out of trouble attaching animals
to their woodland shadows, thereby contemplating
the stuff of the origins of good and evil.
Master Hauggins completes his masterpiece,
Persons of Apparently Little or No Peerage,
yet remains self-abnegating, protesting gently
we oughtn't have named our plan after him.
A.J. and Grace move to Rome.
Valerie and John come home.
Guy reenacts for Bjorn a battle he witnessed

between Bennington, Vermont and Amherst, Massachusetts.
Spencer receives orders to count epiphanies.
Mr. You-Know-Who presents Spencer a hand-held,
stainless steel tally meter to make the job easier.
Spencer appears more confused than ever,
more confused than a beaver
in a waterfall in a shopping mall.
We rule out shopping malls.
Teresa swears off kielbasa, swears by Gertrude Stein.
Alyce teaches the first lady the trick
of a feminized sucker-punch.
Deveraux loses his keys in a 40 acre maze of corn.
Jerry grows little goatees in both of his ears.
Dave Marley and Stephen hitchhike among the great
Sequoia.
Yesho takes London to Turkey to meet the family.
Master Hauggins announces his next topic,
What to Do for Your Friends Marginalized by Fame.
Stuart and Mary spend a splendid evening swimming
in New York City's most glamorous swimming hole.
Claudia and Vernon visit St. Augustine.
Monica and Monique grow up.
Ycola finds it in her heart to forgive her mother
and her father and all of the rest of us.
Uncle Stack lays down his sister-in-law's
wedding bouquet on his brother's grave
and sits down beside them and cries.
Spencer returns Mr. You-Know-Who's tally meter.
It does not bring out the best in either.
Johnny Konik marries too quickly

after his wife suddenly dies.
Lydia fools herself into thinking she can impress
anyone by eating crabs with a knife and fork.
Claire no longer holds it against her long-lost
god-daughter.
Uncle Dude's thirteen kids divide up his land
amongst themselves and stay put.
Aunt Pom's death appears and disappears
like an air mint in her sister's mouth.
Gerard never misses a day without someone
to give him a shave.
Euphrasie spends all afternoon on the porch
untangling her niece's hair.
Cid spots a pair of geese he'll come back
at dusk to shoot.
Marguerite's mind goes up in smoke.
Sister Stephanie is Sister Edward's lover.
Bishop Aloysius excommunicates the racist.
Uncle Richie shakes JFK's hand on Halloween.
And so on and so on, so goes our master plan.

A Lost Pastor

Out of nowhere a raven in a dog collar
appeared to guide me.
But then along came a red-tailed hawk
who got its messages all mixed up.
I evolved into a mole and rooted
through the congregation's lawns.
I grubbed for a living all summer long.
After I'd checked the sopranist's hair
for lice I found myself in danger
of losing my entire fold.
They were drifting away like dandruff.
I'd seen enough and was stuck in a rut.
I knew I needed a fresh start or a new hat.
I lacked will and Will had gotten entangled
with a mailman on the lam. I practically
had no body. And my hair kept falling out
of what little skull I'd managed to keep,
abandoning ship, mutiny amongst the stowaways,
stowaways thick as lice, bugs burrowing tunnels
in my brain furrows.
My turncoat elders recommended
I go in for early retirement or at least
have myself irradiated.
I considered that, much to the dismay
of my acupuncturist, but gave it up
after pouring diesel fuel over my firemaps
and calculating just how far away I lived

from any port. In a storm of self-decoration
I no longer accepted alms.
I accepted hair nets which I employed
to imprison migrating darning needles.
I fed them on lice I'd been fattening
in the sleeping quarters. A few had grown
large as barns. I knew I treaded
on very thin ice. But my Great Aunts
had taken pains to drive it into me.
I was no quitter. Qualms I once embraced
I watched fall through a hole in the ice
where schools of hair-eating fish,
suddenly rich overnight, upset the delicate
balance of their tightly-knit civilization.
They overbuilt and had too many nests
and were threatened with extinction.
Sadly, their one distinction, an absolute lack
of a sense of direction, abandoned them
in the face of so many choices.
Their one hope rested in the tiny hands
of our town officials, an unelected snarl
of two-bit scoundrels who throughout the endless
months of winter never once turned the town fountain off.
It became a saltlick for wounded trucks
and lost caravans of permanently stained saints.
I'd grown strange and tired
of the fish market man and his wife
and the fireman and the firehouse.
I'd become restless, careless, shiftless,
equivocating, cancelling last minute visits

to the sick and dying, failing to report
to funerals and weddings. The formulas
of secret ingredients I'd long guarded
I believed I no longer needed.
They'd be left to generations of better pastors.
Well, everybody's got a compass needle
in a smokestack, a powderkeg in a tinderbox,
a little bit of heresay, a headful of gossip,
a gimmick, a spit curl, a demographic, a statistic.
I'm sending memorial donations directly
to my favorite charity. It's just good business,
a little bird told me.

Resolution

Stop climbing trees.
Stay away from full and empty caves.
Don't even think about caves.
Go out of your way to avoid running after trains.
Sleep like a rock on a rock
high above the timberline.
When morning comes around
roll out of bed and hum
the little notes you know.
Declare your love of mites.
You call this living?
Leave nothing out.
Everything is everywhere
and everybody knows it.
Don't ask panhandlers for change.
Rearrange the hands from the compass
to the clock.
Worry yourself sick.
Take bad advice to the bank.
Figure out who put the treasure in the maze.
Tie a thin line of pure silk
onto the tail of an ant.
Fix yourself a strong drink,
sit in the driveway and wait.

Certification Cereal

The house in which this took place
was the house of the president dummy.

I was a guest in the house
and to be one I had had to pay dearly.

The insurance policy on the house
says its occupants must be tough

rubber dummies ignoring how badly
they're in need of resuscitation.

The house maintains this hypnotic state
because it is decorated with more details

than any dummy can count.
I counted at least three different size dummies.

Are they dying again, or already dead?
Many people say they would like to die in their sleep.

I don't know if this keeps them awake.
Many say they could have died laughing.

So they have already died
but it could not have been

while anything funny was happening.
I would like to sleep in the right size bed

and eat my supper from a bowl I'm big enough to hold.
I would never ask a bear to give me his chair.

The dummy being president
could only have been beside the point

because he, in fact, had been elected president.
Had he not been

it could not have been
beside the point that he was.

Once I was sent to buy milk for the president's
porridge I'd eaten.

I passed a wreck in which no one was hurt.
One of the vehicles resembled a zebra.

The other passed itself off
as a mildly damaged, angry, tiny, blue wasp.

I felt as if I'd been brought back to life.
So when I'd felt like a dummy

because on this mission I bumped into my children
as if they were passing strangers,

it only lasted a second, because they were laughing.
Once I'd accomplished my mission

I was ready for certification
and could practice on living subjects.

The ones I might save can register to vote
and insure the president's reelection.

What

"I don't have time to work for you, darkling,"
I said. He called me *pet* and hired me on the spot.
A storm had drowned the highways in stormy waters.
I was lost, looking for you, hired against my will
by a man who expected me to see to every little detail
of his upcoming coronation. "Opportunity,"
he said, "always knocks twice. Get with the program,
cut your losses, don't look back, crack me some ice."

I was lost, searching for you in the interior,
finding nothing to piece together. I felt you'd gone
for good, foresaken me for something I did or didn't
do. Was there some kind of misunderstanding?
The shopkeepers had locked up their shops.
I feared I'd be mistaken for a looter.
From a redundantly dressed Sister of Mercy
I borrowed a crisp disguise.

I went on about my business, looking for you
in the overcrowded bee-box complex, flooded,
under evacuation orders. I reported to one of the
natives, confessing I didn't vote in his district.
He glanced at me with pity in his distracted eyes
and suggested I leave well enough alone.
Without you I could not imagine going on.
I asked him for a ride, looking past the busloads

of hopeless evacuees, hoping to locate you
who'd always been tricky to find, unpredictable
as the weather. I'd reached a state of panic.
Everywhere I turned blank-eyed men and women wept
in private dismay. Words, torn like leaves
from trees, filled the sky with hideous approbations.
Don't miss your water; water was everywhere,
better light one candle; not a candle to be had.

Curse the darkness until your well runs dry.
I could not find you and feared I'd never find you
again. How would I recognize you? Our paths
might never cross. "My boss would never agree
to let me work," said my private eye, said she.
After what seemed like a lifetime, a nightmare,
a cold eye in an otherwise clockwise storm,
finally when I least expected it, when I'd despaired

and cried out and hidden my cries, out of the blue
you called me. I told you the dog had started talking.
Her first words were (now here's a wide-open window,
a wide-open double French door, a moment to be had
for the having, love requited, all forgiven, nothing
hyphenated, no accidents, no killings, no spills,
no misses, nothing forbidden, no second-guessing,
no revision, options open, electives limitless,

start at the beginning). I swore I'd done nothing
to encourage her. She was insistent and articulate
and I did not understand it. She enunciated clearly,

whispering talk, talk, talk to me, now tell me
what I've been saying.   Neither you nor I denied it.
We agreed to make the best of it, take all we have
and what we might be given, take good care of her
and get on with living.

From My House to Yours

The village store closed for good
and just as suddenly opened its doors.
We go tiptoeingly slow over invisible salamanders

who nevertheless merit our affection
and by virtue of gradual accumulation
work their ways deep into our answers

and our questions. Will anyone buy enough
nightcrawlers to put a dent in that old lady's rent?
There's evidence her sons labor all summer

to sell cordwood in the fall. A crooked window
protects her bathtub Virgin Mary shrine.
Nobody would buy the pink house which in late
                              summer

fairly glowed. Will anyone buy it now
it's painted white? I resist speeding down
the stretch of open road. Everyone knows

a cop's staked himself in the hidden entrance
to the wildlife sanctuary. His blue light waits
to explode. Honeybees are as deaf as stones.

They cruise through their lives virtually unaffected
by blues. I want to get to your house

without disturbing nature or the dead from their
                                        slumber.

Coyotes like this road and have been accused,
like good coyotes everywhere, of killing domesticated
animals. A little farther on comes a place

to have one's fingers painted. I hear there's
a long line for an appointment.
I often think of my collection of kitchen knives

and good advice, the kind worth taking, tells us
dull knives are most dangerous.
Somedays buying duck eggs seems like a good idea.

Then I remember their blood orange yolks.
By now I know the road by heart. I can drive it
in my sleep. And we're reminded daily by the modest

dairy farm that they've invested in the Breed
of the Future. And what breed is that?
There's the majestic maple to look forward to

in the fall. I like the house with many capital Bs
painted on its shutters. Near the community
swimming hole one lonely pony stands solemnly still

in its miniature pen. Signs of life at the tiny
trailer park, the whole place is up for sale.
One tenant's stood a life-size deer in the meadow brush

where it's fooled me more than once.
The cemetery hasn't been used for years.
At last I take the turn into your side road,

all jagged shade, hopping lights and cool shadows.
And when we close the door behind us what
goes on goes on, goes on, goes on, goes on between us.

Anything of Mine You Find Is Yours

I'll go run look between the butter
and oysters. You might look back
beneath the earthen dam and bug-eaten
music. I've already been from A
to I Am Going Home to Mother.
I'll pass on Gothic Street.
Don't overlook your pockets.
I won't forget the trunks, files,
lockers, baskets, bushels, crates,
closets, cupboards, tins, cabinets,
bags, old purses or lock boxes.
It won't take more than a minute.
I'll see to the holes in the hammock,
shifting light on our knickknacks.
You run through the channels.
I'll peer into the dustfree grooves
between decades. You think about
tomorrow. You look over your glasses.
If you find me drifting off to examine
the furrows near your ears and nape,
the great expanse from shoulder to hip,
remind me to forget my work, tell me
to stop all this, put your hand on my head,
encourage me to rest.

Homage to My Chronographer

For you, a flock of diamond doves
pinned itself to the sundial.
How slowly waterclocks evaporate history.
For you, our little mimics' beaks sip,
say, six minutes to six, all around the clock.
Somedays there are worlds to say,
all the time in the world and no words
equal to the task. Language behaves like a maze
within a maze with a mind of its own.
There's no equivalent to time spent, no retrial,
no recompense. Who is the mayor of this town?
This town has no mayor, no lord, no master.

Empathy attaches us to one another tightly.
Time drives this into me directly.
For you, that's what ageratum and geranium say
congregated around the clock, dawdling
around the peaceful borders.
And I, I'm ashamed for every time I've said less
than you deserve.
For you, an unconscious traveler stops and stands
and stares into your history, your destiny, beholding
you the way the world's all-time-greatest surgeon,
seconds before he begins an operation, beholds

an unbroken chest.

Do you believe Pandora's Box filled us with hope?
And whatever happened to Oedipus Rex?
Your laughter interrupts every soggy quotidian.
Your laughter introduces misunderstanding
wherever we need it most.
Every morning fog lifts from the water's
still, mercurial surface.
Matteo Ricci left us blueprints for his Memory Palace.
I hope someone remembers him.
His ghost lives in a blue bottle
filling with rainwater under the Russian Olives.
A sweat bee's inside it, gasping for breath.

For you, I study my senseless wrist,
a bracelet of words I meant to say.
For you, I provide an ambitious guest.
Time rakes waves over the ultra-wide waters
we row from cradle to grave.
Is there a lady ruling this lake?
Immortality-a-go-go's grass widow host?
For you devils will swim
in holy water basins.
The artist of the beautiful grows weary
of fixing clocks. Terror flies from his fingers.
Time never breaks a promise.

One Hand Short

Everyone was crying and weeping
and giggling like little girls
and boys say they do when they see
grown-up lovers kissing.
During the procession I teetered
and wobbled over the train track
I picked for us to walk at dusk.
Had I known the Express ran
through at 5:06?
To be honest with you,
my feelings swayed.
And that you would have liked.
To be honest with you,
I suspect bodies do better
when they up and combust.
My feelings left my body
without much thought.
And now we press a few petals
into the old family Bible
and stare like cattle
over the lives we've collected.
Because it was my body, unmoved
by inspirational passages
I'd selected, I called it
my funeral. Once again, perhaps,
getting it wrong. I knew all along,
as alive as anyone alive,

I couldn't be dead
but I played along.
Figurines hovered over the corpse,
anxious as burnt toast.
By now, I've noticed the smell
of narcissus can easily be mistaken
for the slow burn of electrical fire.
It's disturbing.
I'm the one who should have been smoking.

Reflections Upons Sitting Along with a Friend, for an Itinerant Painter, Manitoba, 1938

At first I thought my Sunday suit
might be much too much,

in harvest wheat, in the stiff,
rough-cut Friday field.

To pass the time I touched
the links of golden chain

my father handed down for me,
careless boy by a rank pond,

to stay in touch with him.
He's long gone.

I inherited the gloom,
jarring in the sun's unlocked, generous

light. Anyone else in the world
would look as oddly cast

as I, cross-legged, slack,
inured. The women laughed

at our straw hats, at odds

with our starched vests and shirts.

They made light of our darker thoughts
until my friend, no slouch,

threw his coat to the wind.
He kindly lent his ease to me.

My father's touch was light,
thin, though it hung

in my throat, my heart, my liver
and my lungs. They like to say

I'm his spitting image.
To me I looked more the stern

landowner I'd become.
My mother's grave sits just beyond that hill.

One would have to lean up close,
and taste the inside of my inner ear,

to know it, how my grievous silence
could be broken by the memory

of water pouring against stone.
I wanted my father then,

younger than I've ever been,
to see me now.

Effects of Tropical Light on the White Man

"When you fail to clean the carrion
off your whiskers, you can expect a passel
of flies." Is that any way to talk
to a cat? I adored foundlings and orphans,
especially orphan emotions. These I found
eager to accept affection, readily tamed,
without expectation, without memories.
Would they eventually feel at home?
And though, I hate to think it,
would they amount to anything after all?
They filled me with gratitude when I sang
to them gently. In my spare time I was
a middle-of-the-road novelist who aspired
to repair the potholes memory made—
in the dentist's chair, at railroad crossings,
as passengers lumbered home for the evening,
in the lulls between thunder and lightning.
I'd bought into a habitat and over the decades
slowly introduced into camouflaged landscapes
previously unacquainted emotions.
Shade for the exhausted, water for the sly,
caves and nooks and crannies for the shy.
Wouldn't all of their bad habits eventually
be absorbed by life's necessities?
There wasn't room for the luxuries
of bickering and backbiting and bad manners,

so these became a thing of the past.
I established a trust to insure well
into the future the welfare of my mission.
It amounted to a drop in the bucket,
but I wouldn't live to see it.
So much unfinished business.
And whose specialty is that?
And why so many questions?
In bad taste on gruesome occasions
legions of unwilling recruits arrived
by ship, under cover of darkness
to lend a semblance of sincerity
to the practice of my target questions.
Toothpicks and spoons and tongs
worked their magical attractions.
Sentences went begging for morsels of endings.
My tenderest inclinations blossomed
over my parenthetical children.
I enjoyed a proud satisfaction
in the Shaker-inspired dormitory
I built for the feeble of mind.
Instructions included limp before the lame,
a sorry piece of a long list I considered
necessary under my obscure circumstances.
I hired self-duplicates to bottle-feed
my pets aromatic teas, teas I traveled
the world to sample. This took me away
for months on end and I'd complain when
I returned how lonely it all had been,
how sad to travel the world all alone.

No Clue

Circumspection, insinuation,
hindsight, hereafter, hero,

ironing out fresh wrinkles,
freshening up sour bedding,

an inkling, digging into
phototherapy, mesmerizing

busy signals, taking up
the french horn,

joining legions of migrating
principles, counting the body's

loopholes' keyholes, holding
everyone's head high,

swelling out like a street banner,
a shambles, a ruin,

a career opportunity for the unborn,
tracking ruts in a tit-for-tat,

tracing dots between trade-offs,
like intoxicated rats in traffic,

kneebent before the crestfallen,
on bended knee over past history,

sifting through unclaimed rubble,
rummaging in sacks

of eggs for singing snakes
or birds, resembling little

the thing we'd set
our hearts upon and cracked.

The Long Story

Sometime later he said
I want to rot in your arms.

The mind/body question
resolved itself finally.

I could no longer name
the subspecies of American cars.

He said I love your flowers.
Great numbers of precious species

went extinct. He said I still will
love you forever deeply.

Summers raced to sunnier lands.
He said he loved me dearly.

Who knows sincerely about sincerity?
He said he loved me, clearly.

He said he loved me madly.
A few leaves had peaked.

All in a Day's Work

Even our children had things to say
about the death penalty,

about executing authority,
about how close to reality they came

to punching out one another's lights.
I couldn't help but hold back a tear

when our son said he loved streetbanners
no matter how they read.

"To dig a hole in the middle of City Park,
to burn yourself up, is it legal?"

It's your life, our daughter remarks,
you can take it any way you want.

All's clear just about then.
Mrs. Frog's all settled in the Inn.

As we recall, Mr. Frog's gone around the bend.
Everyone was in a big rush

to join the soccer casualties of America.
Nobody was listening to anybody.

We looked at one another meaningfully.

The carnivores had located their suppers.
The herbivores gazed across the empty range.

The Cubist Rotisserie

You're living with an elephant
and pretending you aren't.
Dr. Harsh strikes a stern bedside manner
then he fumbles and drops his hammer.
He's shocked at first, embarrassed,
but he quickly recovers in a fit of giggles
and then he confesses.
Dr. Harsh just hates poetry,
"The Emperor of Ice Cream," especially.
You've just felt the second gold bead,
about the size of a seed pearl or split
shot sinker settle in your skull,
the next and last one still to come.
On a panic scale this registers 7.1.
Your elephant's as white as a blizzard
falling through fog onto snowy ground.
Dr. Harsh's thankful his wife's career's in shoes.
He hates to mention the four screws.
It's Pearl Harbor Day and the visiting physicians
who've come to observe speak just Japanese.
Dr. Harsh's machinists have fashioned
a few apertures and targets especially for you.
But first there's the matter of the screws.
"If only man's mind could be seized and held still!"
Your elephant's surprisingly studious
with a deepening interest in the scholastics

and a penchant for quoting St. Augustine.
Dr. Harsh invites you to climb on board
his Star Machine. Exceptionally strong magnets
keep the protons you'll be experiencing contained
in an ever-widening spiral about the size
of a pencil. They'll come at you half
the speed of light, traveling twenty-five miles.
Now your elephant's really got his thinking cap
screwed on tight. He's gotten fond of repeating
himself and feels perfectly free to paraphrase.
"But if only your mind could be seized and held steady,
you would be still for a while, and for that
short moment, you could glimpse the splendor
of eternity." You had no idea, even with his
                                                immense
size, how quickly an elephant becomes a pedant.
Dr. Harsh is hard-nosed, all business, and just
like his non-English speaking guests, he's curiously
courteous. He takes your hand like a knight-errant.
Your head-holder to which your head is attached,
along with your head, or vice versa, is hitched
to a rotating frame. There's no getting out of it,
it's time to feed the elephant, and no one to blame.

The Soup Drill

The time it takes certain fashions to change,
say, togas to pantaloons, wigs to pierced nipples,
correlates inversely to the time it takes to bore
a handful of holes into an icecube of pesto.
Some ideas last about as long as it takes frozen
soup to defrost. Cowpokes like to yodel on about
how much easier it is to break an unbroken colt.
Fact is, going on the last fifty years, rustlers
mostly work out of helicopters.
Time was, every other rustler's mother committed
to memory her old family remedies.
Who do I think put the stars up there?
What do I think the ladle is for?

Without a Similar Condition
Including this Condition

The farther away from the center of power
you build your house

the longer your light bulbs will last.
An electrician told me.

Through fog, through buds
and leaves touched with red

before they turn colors
I ponder the blind horse

as it follows the flanks of its mate
through the pasture.

The horse with good eyes
grazes.

I've never seen it run.
The blind horse keeps its head

never more than a few feet away
from its friend.

Anonymous

Anonymous fits the description,
so clear, so not there.

Anonymous can't get called
on the carpet or taken to the cleaners.

Anonymous learned early on
what fishing for compliments gets.

Anonymous lost the high school election
and never got over it.

Anonymous has an ounce of imagination.
Anonymous is asexual. How can we tell?

Look in any anonymous cell.
Anonymous models for anchorites.

Read anonymous's celebacy will.
Off the record anonymous

has much to say about celebrity.
Anonymous says something is wrong

with anybody not anonymous.
Anonymous wishes fathers had been tougher.

Anonymous despises mothers.
Anonymous calls home every holiday

and every other day anonymous can call.
Anonymous can miss a bus and never miss

an appointment or anybody else.
Erratic, unreliable, manic, anonymous.

Anonymous mistakes earth's gravity
for lunar gravity.

Anonymous could care less.
Anonymous is nostalgic, magnanimous,

miserable, ecstatic, insomniac,
kleptomaniac, narcoleptic.

Anonymous dresses impeccably,
whatever that means.

Anonymous dresses anonymously.
When anonymous gets called for jury duty

anonymous asks for the death penalty.
Egg cannot stick to anonymous's face.

Anonymous breezes through life,
unattached, uninhibited, unvanquished.

Anonymous likes to distinguish
between what's publicly and privately anonymous.

Anonymous gets stuck in traffic.
Anonymous pitches a fit.

Unnamed sources routinely accuse anonymous
of unmentionalbe acts.

Anonymous makes acrobatic leaps
of mental dexterity quite unnecessarily.

Anonymous exercises no respect
for the right to privacy.

Anonymous is the ringer
in ideologies of democracy.

Anonymous is a riot.
Is anonymous for us or against us?

Somewhere among us the anonymous
donor waits to console us.

Recent Titles in the Carnegie Mellon Poetry Series

1995
Germany, Caroline Finkelstein
Housekeeping in a Dream, Laura Kasischke
About Distance, Gregory Djanikian
Wind of the White Dresses, Mekeel McBride
Above the Tree Line, Kathy Mangan
In the Country of Elegies, T. Alan Broughton
Scenes from the Light Years, Anne C. Bromley
Quartet, Angela Ball

1996
Back Roads, Patricia Henley
Dyer's Thistle, Peter Balakian
Beckon, Gillian Conoley
The Parable of Fire, James Reiss
Cold Pluto, Mary Ruefle
Orders of Affection, Arthur Smith
Colander, Michael McFee

1997
Growing Darkness, Growing Light, Jean Valentine
Selected Poems, 1965-1995, Michael Dennis Browne
Your Rightful Childhood: New and Selected Poems, Paula Rankin
Headlands: New and Selected Poems, Jay Meek
Soul Train, Allison Joseph
The Autobiography of a Jukebox, Cornelius Eady
The Patience of the Cloud Photographer, Elizabeth Holmes
Madly in Love, Aliki Barnstone
An Octave Above Thunder: New and Selected Poems, Carol Muske

1998
Yesterday Had a Man in It, Leslie Adrienne Miller
Definition of the Soul, John Skoyles
Dithyrambs, Richard Katrovas
Postal Routes, Elizabeth Kirschner
The Blue Salvages, Wayne Dodd

The Joy Addict, James Harms
Clemency, Colette Inez
Scattering the Ashes, Jeff Friedman
Sacred Conversations, Peter Cooley
Life Among the Trolls, Maura Stanton

1999
Justice, Caroline Finkelstein
Edge of House, Dzvinia Orlowsky
A Thousand Friends of Rain: New & Selected Poems 1976-1998,
        Kim Stafford
The Devil's Child, Fleda Brown Jackson
World as Dictionary, Jesse Lee Kercheval
Vereda Tropical, Ricardo Pau-Llosa
The Museum of the Revolution, Angela Ball
Our Master Plan, Dara Wier